To my stinky pies,
Owen, Craig, and Jillian.

The Science behind

Different Types of Poop

By
Science Kids University

Hi, I'm Miss Poopoo Doodoo. I'm one of the teachers here at Poop Academy.

Second: Your poop changes depending on **what** you eat and drink. It can even be affected by **how much** you eat and drink.

For example, if you don't drink or consume enough water or fiber, you can experience hard poop.

They can be called...

Another type of poop, caterpillar, is long-shaped and lumpy. Here we have another sign of constipation that, again, shouldn't happen frequently.

Hot dogs are long-shaped with some cracks on the surface. This is the gold standard of poop, especially if it's somewhat soft and easy to pass.

Another type of poop, snake, is smooth and snake-like. Doctors also consider this a normal poop that should happen every one to three days.

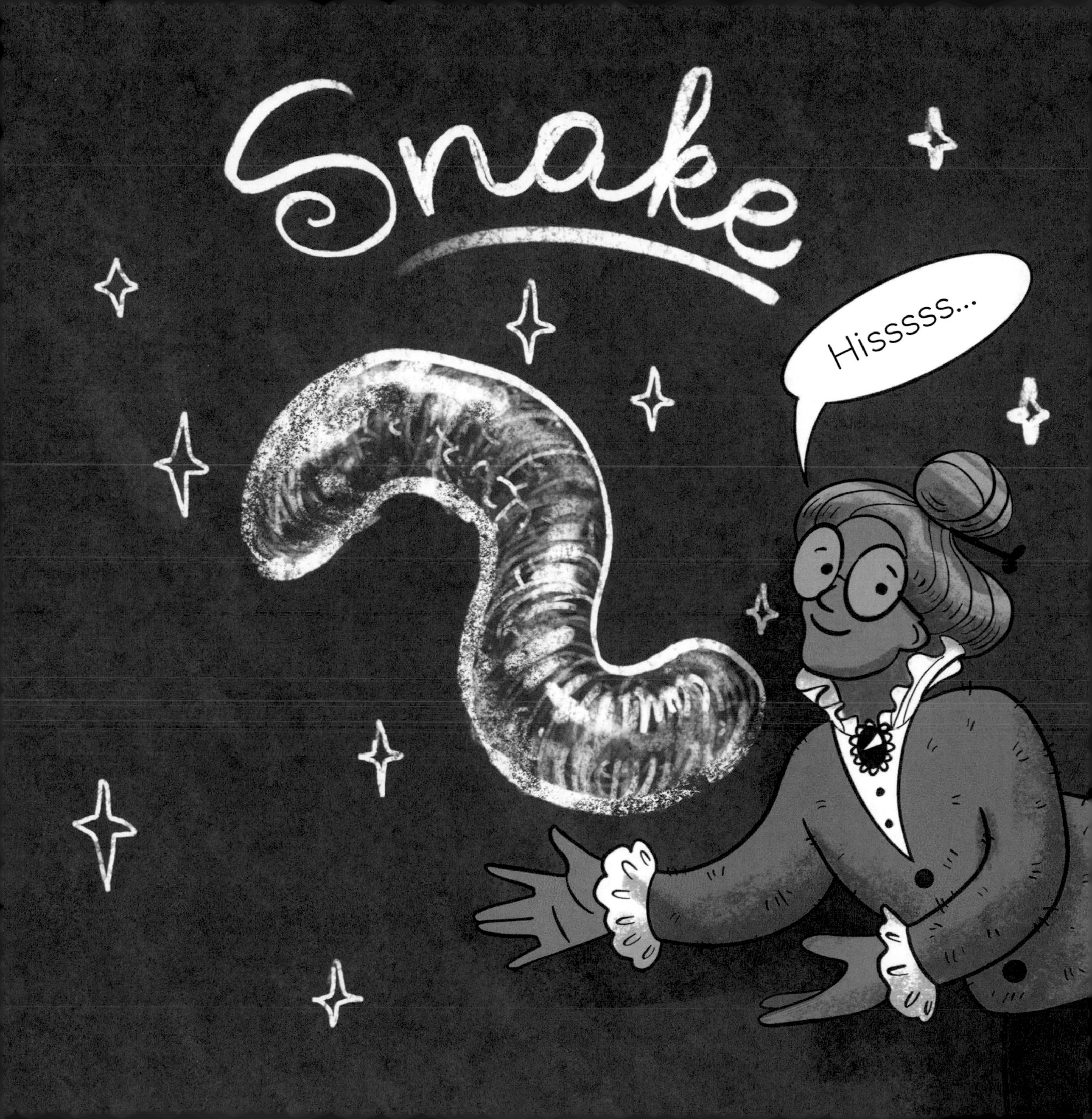
Snake
Hisssss...

Blobs are small, like the first ones, but soft and easy to pass. The blobs also have clear cut edges. This type of poop means you are lacking fiber and should find ways to add some to your diet through vegetables.

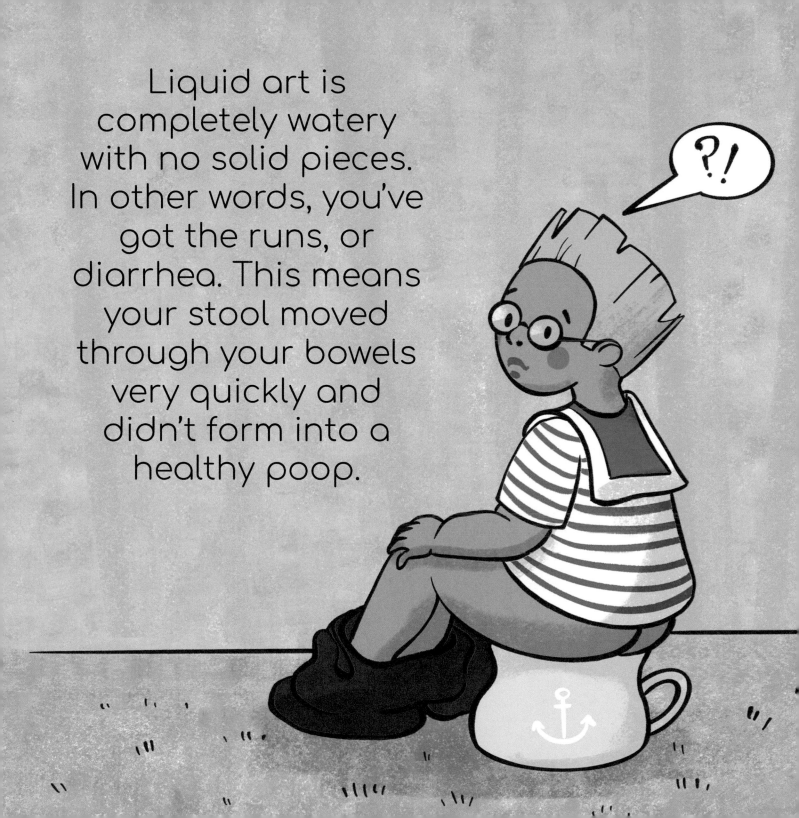

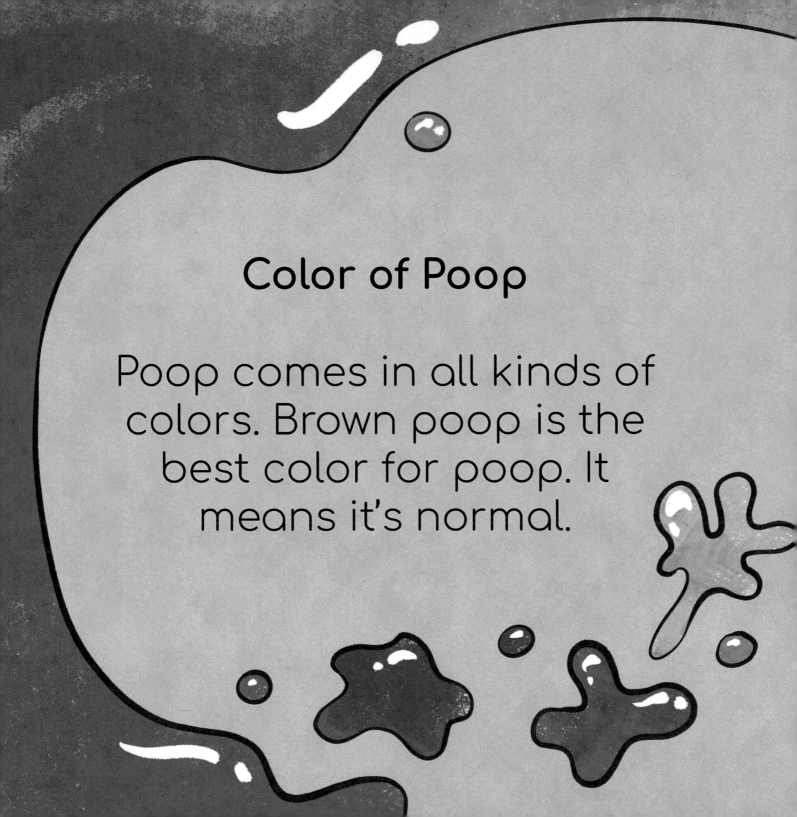

Color of Poop

Poop comes in all kinds of colors. Brown poop is the best color for poop. It means it's normal.

Some people poop in the morning.

Some at school.

Some after dinner.

Some right before bed.

Turn the page for some poop jokes.

That's all for today. The type of poop you have can vary from day to day. Just know it's quite normal to experience different kinds. There's no need to be embarrassed. Stay tuned for our next book...

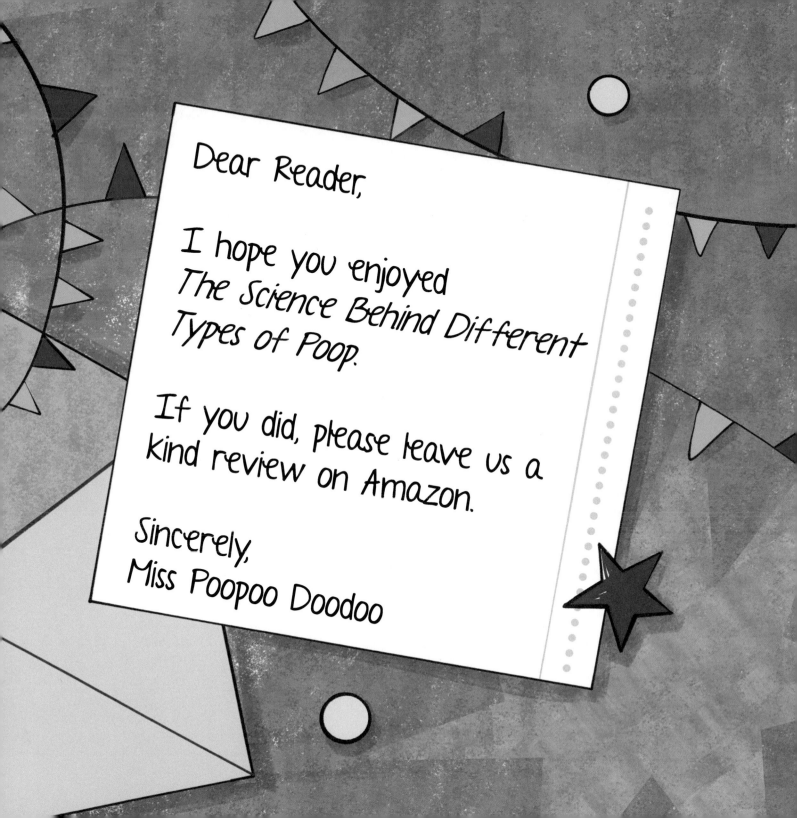

MarBLes

Soft Serve ice cream

Liquid Art

hot dog

Made in the USA
Monee, IL
05 November 2021

Caterpillar

snake